Jesus Merch

A Catalog in Poems

Megan McDermott

Fernwood
PRESS

Jesus Merch

A Catalog in Poems

©2023 by Megan McDermott

Fernwood Press
Newberg, Oregon
www.fernwoodpress.com

Printed in the United States of America

Cover and interior design by Mareesa Fawver Moss

Cover photo by Rock'n Roll Monkey

ISBN 978-1-59498-102-9

Poignancy, humor, and an eccentric array of Christian merch are all to be found in this lovely collection by Megan McDermott. Every poem will make you think, many will make you laugh, and some will settle in your soul. McDermott's poetic eye is finely attuned to the mysterious life of the spirit, even within the oddest of religious signifiers. This poetry reveals the grace behind commercialism and illuminates the paradox of our human hearts, with all "the ways they must love / and break and love again."

Sarah Law
author of *Thérèse: Poems* (Paraclete Press) and
editor-in-chief of *Amethyst Review*

Who'd have thought that profundity could be woven out of kitschy catalogs? Megan McDermott is the high priestess of camp, able to hold earnest baubles aloft, then transubstantiate material goods into spiritual gifts. She nails some killer endings in these poems, which are as entertaining as they are thought-provoking. My heart hurt a little at the end.

Tina Kelley
author of *Rise Wildly* and
Abloom & Awry (CavanKerry Press)

With tenderness and humor, Megan McDermott holds Christian capitalism up to the light in *Jesus Merch*, considering the effects of trademarking "Glory" in a game, the uses and marketing of items from a "JESUS WRECKS SINS" inflatable wrecking ball to Christian Plush Pumpkins to Fantastic Faith Tattoos. The poet asks thoughtful questions of the merchandise, as though in conversation with the physical objects— for example, in "Color Your Own Paul Speaks Boldly Megaphone—$7.29" she asks: "But how do you construct a craft / about sitting still or making space?" From vintage board games to a blow-up Jonah's whale, the attention of this collection is richly curious, playful, and deep-hearted. What a joy to sit with these poems and the poet who muses of a Let's Be Christian Soldiers coloring book, "Joan, the saint / I would date if I had / to date a saint."

Han VanderHart
author of *What Pecan Light* (Bull City Press)
and editor of *Moist Poetry Journal*

To all those who have relied on the lifelines of creativity and literature in times of loneliness,

and to all who have desired something greater than the companionship of poems.

Contents

Acknowledgments

Thanks to the following publications which have published these poems in earlier versions:

Amethyst Review: "Giant Inflatable Whale—$19.59,"
    "Heavenly Scene Backdrop Banner—$10.37"

Earth & Altar: "Jesus Has a Pizza My Heart
    Notepads—$7.19," "Fantastic Faith Tattoos—$2.57,"
    "Kid's Prayer Boredom Buster Kit—$39.99," "Plush
    Autograph Cross—$4.39"

EcoTheo Review: "Upright Tower"

Eight Poems Journal: "Little Boolievers Mini Playing
    Cards—$8.39"

Fare Forward: "A Variety of Christian Pumpkins"

Miniskirt Magazine: "Religious Valentine Conversation
    Heart Scented Erasers—$3.47"

Moist Poetry Journal: "Let's Be Christian Soldiers: Activity
    and Coloring Book—1950s

Neologism Poetry Journal: "2020 Religious Water Color
    Calendar—$1.07"

Night Coffee Lit: "Jonah & the Whale Sign Craft Kit—$9.99"

Presence: A Journal of Catholic Poetry: "Noah's Ark Twisty Puzzles—$11.27"

Rogue Agent Journal: "Faith Arrow Sign—$11.09"

Stirring: A Literary Collection: "Vintage Bible Battles Card Game—1970s"

Thimble Literary Magazine: "Jesus' Miracles Mystery Scratch N' Reveal Cards—$9.49"

Author's Note

Poems in this collection take their titles from three main sources. Items with a price listed, rather than a decade or a year, are contemporary items found on-line through Orientaltrading.com under the heading "Religious Items." In the 1930s, Oriental Trading was founded by Japanese immigrant Henry Watanabe with a focus on small items for parties and carnivals. Eventually the business expanded, offering a variety of affordable items for settings such as Sunday School classes and church events, as well as religious gifts and decor. Items specifying origins in the twentieth century, including Sunday School items and Christian games, were found through Etsy and Ebay listings. Victorian and Georgian-era board games were all found in the book *Georgian and Victorian Board Games: The Liman Collection*, which brings together items displayed in an exhibit at the Yale British Art Center.

I.

Inflatable Construction VBS
Wrecking Ball—$19.99

A cross hovers above
the words "JESUS WRECKS
SIN," and I wonder how the game
is played—who aims
and who's the object. Does one
boisterous child volunteer
to play "SIN," or do most
perform the role, darting
away, falling into grass,
laughing when hit? Will
they remember this game later
as they pray that Jesus might
knock them over for real?

I really don't begrudge Jesus his wrecking.
My confusion is about how and when
and whether one should really
approach it with glee.

An honest prayer would find me
letting out the wrecking ball's air,
honoring anyone whose faith
became examining horizons,
waiting for judgment
to swing into sight.

A Variety of Christian Pumpkins

Christian Plush Pumpkins—$19.99
Christian Pumpkin Crinkle Tissue Paper Craft Kit—$9.99
Christians Are Like Pumpkins Sign Craft Kit—$9.69
Pin the Cross on the Pumpkin Halloween Game—$4.89
Christian Pumpkin Keychains—$3.97
Christian Pumpkin Bowling Game—$12.49

And more.

There is no story I've ever learned
about Jesus and the pumpkin patch.
He cursed fig trees, plucked wheat,
used mustard seed as metaphor,
called himself bread, created
wine, but nothing pumpkin.
If there are Christian pumpkins,

are there also Buddhist ones
and Sihk and Muslim and Jewish
and Hindu and Bahai ones?
Atheist and agnostic pumpkins?
Some that are spiritual but not religious?

How does the Christian pumpkin
show its Christian-ness?

According to the pictures,
a pumpkin communicates faith
through a carved cross,
candle glowing
in its emptied body.

Conceding the possibility
of its existence, let me ask:
Can a Christian pumpkin ever
just be whole? Unmarred,
uninterrupted orange?
Not standing out but just
a pumpkin among pumpkins,
doing pumpkin-hood well?
A pumpkin not lit for our
benefit but somehow
alight for its own brethren, giving
off some gourdian version
of mercy and praise?

A pumpkin's testimony, something like this:
I took in the sun, and I grew,
just like he asked me to.

THOU SHALT NOT: Vintage Sunday School Flannelgraph Religious Ephemera— 1940s

Though the tablets
divide into "SHALL"
and "SHALT NOT,"
they're both topped
with a grumpy stone
face, the tone of
"NOT" allowed
to overtake everything.
Why can't the tablets
be carved with hearts,
Moses' initials plus
the tetragram? Yes,
they will be thrown
regardless. Rules
shattering, needing
re-etching. Which
makes hearts even
more appropriate,
the ways they must love
and break and love again.

Noah's Ark Twisty Puzzles—$11.27

Now this could've been useful
way back when. Imagine being trapped
between ark walls, trapped with animals
you normally would've never let
inside, their sounds, their stench,
not to mention a family flipping
between squabbles and silence.
You would need something else
to look at occasionally, besides
carcasses in the water. Often
you'd catch one in your peripheral
vision and begin thinking it must
be a neighbor or a childhood friend.
Finally allowing yourself to turn,
then it would already be past recognition.
Again you'd find yourself churning
from something more than the sea.
You would need something to hold
in your hands, which were kept busy
so long with construction. Your hands,
which had nothing more to make.
The saved saved, the doomed doomed.
But they could still know prayer
through movement. You'd twist
the little cartoon animals and ask
God that somehow this violence,
despite sense, might align into cheeriness,
something as cute as this.

Jonah's Journey Board Game—1970s

The finish line is Nineveh,
though that is where
the real trouble begins.
Where you get enveloped
by existential angst rather
than whale stomach. Where
you create your own churning
waters through selfishness
or maybe trauma. After
the finish line is a bush,
which shades then withers.
I can't be mad at the game
ending where it ends. Sometimes
we all need victories called early.

Giant Inflatable Whale—$19.59

*"Use this giant ocean pal as part of your Jonah And
The Whale lessons or have him make a splash at any
Sunday School or VBS event."*

The "or"
is what interests me,
a whale able to play
two roles: either
Jonah's doom-slash-
savior (doom because
who wants to be
stuck in whale
insides, savior
because it was dry,
it wasn't drowning,
wasn't death)
or just some generic
example of God's
creation to be
dragged out of
the closet for any
old event.

Though on some level,
maybe it makes sense
to play both roles at once.
Jonah's whale wouldn't
define herself by Jonah,
who was just a bit of odd food
she couldn't digest, a footnote.

If the whale were being used
by God, then it didn't know it.
What, then, of the whale's own graces,
things for which we have no record?

A New and Moral Entertaining Game
of The Reward of Merit—1801

"12. a Pious Child

Take up a stake, you will be blest,
Because you pray, and Sin detest."

What if your prayer made itself
tangible as you knelt in your bedroom?
A cloud of smoke spinning
out fervent lips? What if
you could reach in? Would
there be something to grab, take?
I want vaccines and confessions
of love, a few weeks' vacation,
a hug. Could God's hand
be there if you press your own
far enough in, if you don't
mind the mist and the fact
you can't see where you're going?
Prayer is a reaching in,
followed by more reaching.
And when you pull your hand
out, unsure if it met anything
in that space and unsure
if the space was real,
will you then find a game piece
in your upturned palm? Will
you find yourself a step
closer to whatever your life
might win you?

Jesus' Miracles Mystery
Scratch N' Reveal Cards—$9.49

In the place where the miracle
is supposed to be,
there is a hole.

You can see Jesus,
the crowds, water,
but you cannot see
the whole scene
until you become
a participant yourself—

scratching, violent, against surfaces
so something counterintuitive might be revealed,

otherwise known as praying.

Bulk Long Arm Plush Angels, 72 pc.—$99.99

I don't like the *Chicken Soup* version,
angels selective in car wreck rescue

while the unchosen head to the morgue.
And yet I say I believe. Maybe I'd believe

better if I pictured them this way, hands
padded with velcro, arms wider

than the showy wings we think make angels
angels though arms are what serve and hold.

Have angel arms ever enveloped me
in moments when my anxious body

might otherwise have crumbled? Hands
pressed together for the long haul, as if

by velcro. Their arms this plush, lacking
all muscle but—that endless softness.

True Story Adult's Christmas T-Shirt—$9.99

The words "True Story"
are nestled underneath a manger,

and I wonder how that is supposed
to mean anything to anyone other

than the wearer. Though maybe
the lack of further argument

says something in and of itself:
faith is saying, "True story,"

while knowing afterward
you'll draw a blank,

unable to provide convincing
proof beyond your gut's

insisting, *This is what I—*
somehow—know.

Vintage Box Life of Jesus Bible Flash Cards—1984

"Jesus was on the _____ when He asked
the Father to forgive...."

I. run

It was the responsible,
thing to do as they sought
his life and breath
and being, all God-given
goods. So he whispered
mercies over his shoulder
at shrinking enemies. Why
would forgiveness mean
that he must break?

II. phone

Sure, maybe that's not
how prayer works for us,
but Jesus is special,
not having to rely on
mutters met with silence,
but instead God's direct
line. Sprawled out on his bed
at mother Mary's, legs
kicked up as he cradled
phone between ear and
shoulder. There was a sigh

on the other end. "Jesus,
you know I always do."

III. mend

The divinity in him
refused death, ushered
in more breath than
the cross could take
away. Instead of dying,
he stepped down simply,
shook his head, recovered
as if from a hangover.

IV. cross

This is what the blank was waiting for.
What the world was waiting for?
"Cross," a child is expected
to say. "Cross," meant to rise,
perfunctory, from the lips.
Thank God for this distant kind
of violence, that we execute
now in other ways. Injections
and electric chairs, shots fired
in a street, school, or mall,
political neglect. The unique-
ness helps somehow. But
only for us. The feeling
of death the same as ever
in Jesus' chest. The forgiveness
just as much of a stretch.

Plush Autograph Cross—$4.39

"Instead of guestbook, use this Plush Autograph
Cross! It's a perfect addition to supplies for a party
after a baptism, First Communion, and other
sacraments, and it's great at other celebrations,
too...."

The cross invites my name.
The cross soft and meant
for sentiment, for centering
a milestone of someone-
other-than-Christ. Is this
desecration or just a serious
belief in "Good Friday" good-
ness? The cross so transformed,
why shouldn't it be plush instead
of wood? So encompassing
that every name can find
a place on it, accompanied
by Sharpie smiles.

3D Fiery Furnace Craft Kit—$12.49

Here, children, is a story of burning.
Well, a story of *not* burning.
Of God making invincible.
A story saying there might
be a day where someone
wants to throw you
into a fire, but God
will side with you.

Where is the story that tells us
not to be the ones pushing
others into flames?
Or do we have to settle
for the lesson being implied?

Give me a craft kit
where Nebuchadnezzer
realizes the depths
of his sin beforehand
and doesn't require God's
showy miracles or
where a guard begins
to bind but instead
intervenes, without first
being proven wrong by power.

Color Your Own Paul Speaks Boldly
Megaphones—$7.29

What about the shy kids? The quiet
ones? How will they feel hearing
that holiness is loud? That faith
is about letting your voice carry,
being the one in the know,
or having something to give? Nobody
remembers Paul for his listening.
Though the ones who listen often
form us more than our preachers.
But how do you construct a craft
about sitting still or making space?
We have to show how to take turns—
picking up megaphones, putting them down.

Color Your Own Mary or Martha Posters—$3.57

On one side, Jesus and Mary
both smile. On the other,
Martha scowls and stirs. All
under the ominous banner,
"Are you Mary or Martha?"
This is the gospel of grinning—
good Christian women deemed
good for positivity more than
anything else. Could Mary
be a Mary all the time? Would
she even recognize her sister
in caricature, or would she know
that grimace as only one side
of the thousands shown
in intertwined lives? Martha,
the sister who held her, the sister
who laughed. Neither intended
to become a paradigm.

The Mansion of Bliss, A New Game for the Amusement of Youth—1822

"17. REPENTANT PRODIGAL

Thou'rt welcome again to this home,
I felt for and pitied thy fate;
Two counters receive from the bank,
I'm glad thou return'st not too late."

A note of threat in that last line:
that is how you make a parable

a game. Mercy a twist of good
fortune rather than being's ground.

"Repentant prodigal" something
to be played at, landed on, maybe

skipped over. I don't know
the rules for sure. Is repentance

necessary for a win? Presumably
the older brother, devoted and jaded,

already stands inside the mansion
but without the feeling of victory.

Emoji Angel Necklaces—$4.37

A symbol around my neck to say
I'm innocent but modern,
heavenly but hip,
unthreatening in
my holiness.

Angels in scripture always
seem to provoke fear
before telling trembling
humans to chill out.
It's that quality of
otherworldliness
we so often leave
on the angelic cutting
room floor.

We make angels just like
smilies, so easy
to drop into a text or
put on a chain, to
make small.

I want to wear an angel,
but maybe she'd better wear me,
strap me to just one feather
of unfurling, monstrous wings.

Heavenly Scene Backdrop Banner—$10.37

Clouds, beams of light—
the classics.

I've sometimes been afraid
of heaven, and this is
the heaven of my fear—
an eternity encapsulated
in something unnatural,
static, and devoid of heart.

Who wants to live in the air?

Still, the Bible has a few
other images: cities
and banquets and rivers,
things I've known,
things that feel human.
But they don't dilute
the fear of forever.

Any image is still a grasping
at something my hands have never held.

Rare Vintage "GLORY" Christian Bible Board Game—1980s

> *"OBJECT OF THE GAME....As the name implies, the object of the game is to enter 'GLORY ™' and be with the Lord. It could be said the first person that reaches GLORY ™ wins....however, everyone will arrive in GLORY ™ at the end of the game!"*

I can appreciate a theology
where no one wins. Or everyone wins,
and no one loses. Last will be first
and all of that. Every gamer gaining
glory. But what does it mean for
the glory you enter to be trademarked?
Everything in glory a franchise,
logo-emblazoned. Heavenly banquet
your fast food of choice, angels
decked in robes from your go-to
department store. Where are the small
Etsy shops of glory? The Patreons?
The poets? Those who can only
afford to type "™" but not do it?
Glory homemade and crafty?
Hobby glory, from de-stressed
hands, unwound minds? I'm seeking
a sneaking lowercase glory, quiet
melodies of God underneath the blaring
thrum of corporate heaven.

Rare Jesus Spinner Board Game
"Birth and Boyhood of Jesus"—1950s

Only canonical scenes
included. No infancy Gospel
of Thomas with its brutality,
though brutality remains.
Remember Joseph and Mary
realizing Jesus was not with them,
Jesus' upbraiding response:
"Why were you searching
for me? Did you not know...?"
The one doing the spinning
can decide: Is the brutality
a son's indifference—the dagger
of prioritizing another Father—
or instead, is it all the things
a parent, even in their love,
might refuse to know?

Bible Match-a-Verse Game—
Book of Matthew—1950s

"Matthew 1:21—And she shall bring forth a _____...."

A novel. A poetry collection. A degree
in biochemistry. A perfect cartwheel.
A vegan dinner. A petition
with a thousand signatures. A biting
political argument. A full-time job
with benefits. A consensus.
A revelation. A fight. A frown.
So many possibilities dwelled
within her. And/or there are
so many things God could've
gifted her instead. Things she may
have wanted more or less.
But who knows what she
desired? What fills the blank
is enough to cast shadow
on any other potential bearing.

Vintage Bible Zoo Game—1954

The goal is guessing
at creatures who appeared
in verses but never a zoo.
A favorite theologian,
Evelyn Underhill, wrote
to C.S. Lewis, "I feel
your concept of God
would be improved
by just a touch of wildness."
In the Bible zoo game,
shouldn't it end with
the zoo's end too? Peace-
able kingdom and all that.
The winner lets down
the doors of the ark.

Little Boolievers Mini Playing Cards—$8.39

"Frankly, I Follow Jesus!"—Frankenstein
"Wrapped In The Love Of Jesus!"—Mummy

Nightmare creatures
removed of nightmare,

given smiles and
proclamation. Creatures

meant to jar and make
us question freed of

questions—granted faith
with exclamation marks.

Where is the angst appropriate
to a cobbled together, not-

meant-to-be man? Or a body
in its burial clothes,

and yet alive enough
to move and haunt?

Both so far from
what we mean when

we say "resurrection."
But maybe that explains it.

Longing to break out of half-lives,
they'll smile at anyone who asks.

Vintage Sunday School Post Cards /
8 Total Unused—1950s

"WANTED
A missing member of our Sunday-school class"

Imagine if this card were true,
and anytime you skipped church,
your own TV might turn against you,
reveal you, your children as "wanted,"
"missing." Imagine that interruptions
might pop up while streaming
whatever you worry is not godly—
Game of Thrones or *Bridgerton* sex scenes,
news that makes you cynical, YouTube
videos of influencers you claim to hate-watch.
The word that comes to mind is "intrusion," but
"intrusion" implies there's something to be violated.
The church might intrude, but does Jesus ever?
All our habits, television and otherwise, laid bare
before him. All the things we've been missing.

Submission Valley*

The people who live there
love saying "yes" and "please"
and "after you." They love
honorifics, formal address,
but only for others, never
themselves, insisting you
call them by their first names,
though never strongly enough
to earn the verb "insisting."
They hold all plans and preferences
loosely—ready to follow the path
of another who shows themselves
more sure. Not much gets done
in the valley, except when
they have visitors willing
to speak their minds and risk
the charge of selfishness. These
outsiders rarely stay once tired
of making all the decisions.
They move home where the burden
gets shared. And those in the valley
gather in their silent churches,
waiting for the voice of One
who needs no other to direct it.

*Title of a space on The Paths of Life board game,
published in 1840

Happy Old Age Hall*

This is what's offered
to the good. Though

haven't the game makers heard
that only the good die young?

That's not true either,
but it is true that there aren't

any guarantees, which I can say
in a poem without hesitation

while still somehow believing
I am owed as close

to eternity as I can get for doing
nothing particularly special.

*Title of a space on The Paths of Life board game,
published in 1840

Vintage "The Game of Traits"
Bible Card Game—1930s

*"It is permissible to have a Bible on the table for
reference in case a player does not know how his
verse should read."*

Gameplay
with a Bible
at hand. Bible
for answers, for
filling gaps, for
winning. Bible
to be used *against.*
Or: Bible for fun,
Bible for levity, for good-
natured ribbing
between competitors
slash friends. Bible as
a Presence, steady
in the background
of laughter.

Set of 4 Vintage Religious/Church "We Missed You in Sunday School" Postcards—1960s

"'Suffer the little children to come unto me'
We missed YOU"

A toddler in a play pen
is gazed at by an inquisitive
white Jesus hung on the nursery
wall. The parents holding
this card might think
about their child's actual
bedroom, whatever hung
there, its lack of Jesus painting.
Did they prefer the bright
thing that lived there instead,
their slow Sunday morning,
cartoons over hymns? Suffer
the little children to play,
to not yet feel guilty.

Keep Jesus In Your Heart
Worry Stones—$13.49

If you don't have locks,
if you don't have a security system,
if you don't have a password,
if you don't have facial
recognition software,
if you don't have bars on windows,
if you don't instill shame,
if you don't say, "If you loved me,
you'd stay," if you don't—

he'll slip out to another
heart that needs him,
that would treat him
better or at least hold
harder to his feet.

Don't you know you need to keep
him still?

Keep him satisfied?

Nativity Journey Christmas Board Game—$3.29

"The first player who reaches
Jesus in the manger wins."

Does the head start go to those baptized as babies,
or are the ones with more dramatic entrances
likely to surge ahead—those with "testimonies"?
And once on the board, what is it that propels?
"An angel brings good news! +2 spaces."
"A sheep is blocking the path. -1 space."
Is it all about dice and spinners, things
out of our control? There are whole theological
systems trying to answer what it means
for someone to make it to Jesus. Today
I want to parse no scripture. I only want
it to be a game, where there is no prize
for winning, and the stakes are low
for losers, and everything is measured
by how many laughs we're able
to fit from here to there.

Vintage Sunday School Poster—1940s

"Learning of Jesus at Home"

"I am reminded of your sincere faith, a faith that lived first in your grandmother Lois and your mother Eunice and now, I am sure, lives in you."—2 Timothy 1:5 (NRSV)

In the poster, a young mother sits
in front of an open window—night
sky, full moon—while her child—
age three, maybe four—kneels
on the ground in front of her, closed
eyes, folded hands. Captured: a moment
of transmission. A mother's faith
blooming in this body that also
bloomed from her own. The poster
recommends a passage from Second
Timothy that speaks of faith passed
generation to generation. Sometimes
this is true. Sometimes we break links.
Sometimes we transform and twist
them. My Catholic parents taught
me to pray, and now I teach others
about prayer as an Episcopal
woman priest. We learn at home
and outside it. We learn at home,
but see, the poster knows: we learn
at home with the window open.

Devotion Grove*

A friend tells me he wants
to be buried under a tree,
so at least in death
he knows he'll contribute
to something's growth.

Devotion *to* the grove,
the dirt that made us.

Will that grove be one
where someone once
snuck a prayer, awed
by light filtered through
branches? And if so, did
the person praying believe
her words seeped
into the soil, that they
might sprout, or was
she directing her thought
beyond the branches?

Perhaps devotion
is more fluid
than focused, ready to
ricochet off of, into,
whatever tree, deer,
moss waits, whatever
life (or lost life, poured-out
life, changed?) nestles
in the nearby ground

inattentive or attentive,
who's to say?

*Title of a space on The Paths of Life board game,
published in 1840*

Upright Tower*

Language of posture,
of morals: upright, good
and crooked, bad. Think:
When is it that the body curves,
bends, ripples? When it dances,
straddles, leans into a kiss;
slouches on the couch
with Netflix playing, curled up
in a nap; whenever the body
most enjoys itself. Upright
is the posture of waiting,
presenting, sometimes
praying or singing, moments
that can hold joy, yes, but—
if they push you toward
the joy that unravels, you
must allow the clean line
of yourself to break; sway,
fall to knees. Towers
play at being invulnerable,
and in that, communicate
the holy, though they may
not be able to receive it.

Title of a space on The Paths of Life *board game,
published in 1840*

Bible Board Game
"The Bible Says....TIS SO"—1960s

"5 POINT PROVERBS....10 POINT PROVERBS....
15 POINT PROVERBS....20 POINT PROVERBS....
25 POINT PROVERBS...."

For five points, know
that wisdom is better
than gold, rubies;
that it loves rebuke.
For ten, the danger
of greed, wickedness,
loans. Fifteen, the need
to avoid boasting, hate.
In the twenty-point
realm, "wine is
a mocker" and "even
a child is known by
its doings." Twenty-five
point proverbs advertise
merits of "a friend
that sticketh closer than
a brother," "a soft answer,"
"a virtuous woman,"
"a good name."

You can rack up the points
if you wish. But first
let me tell you: for no
points, you can know

55

what it feels like to be
unwise or not in the know.
For no points, you can be
obstinate, neglecting advice,
chucking it in favor of whims.
For no points, you might
know a really juicy sin—let
it wreck your life, your parents'
trust, let it lead you to rebuilding,
redefining. For no points, you
can say what you are thinking
and see what happens when
you tell the truth.

II.

500 Fabulous Foam Self-Adhesive Faith Shapes—$9.99

Shapes of faith listed as:
the word "God,"
the word "Jesus,"
crosses, hearts, fish,
hands, church
buildings, and
what I think are
maybe footprints.

In my life, faith
is sometimes shaped
the same: God,
Jesus, church. But
sometimes faith's
shapes are more
amorphous or even
shredded so I can't
make out what used
to be there. But even
when I can't decipher
them, I still peel off
their backing and press
them onto whatever
hollows my heart.
I will take vague
and sloppy as long
as they stick.

Kid's Prayer Boredom Buster Kit—$39.99

Do they mean for prayer to sound like a mere
boredom alleviator? Or does the kit actually aim
to bust open prayer's boring
shell, so it might be felt as something alive?

Either way, the message is
that prayer is fun, colorful, easy,
with inspiring stickers saying,
"Life is fragile! Handle with prayer!"
or "Prayer changes things!"

One voice in me calls
simplicity a concession
to help children understand
while wondering how
we might also prepare them
for the complexity. But another
voice says, God, make it
this simple for me

so that if I were to have a poster
for my own petitions, I could fill in
the "How did God answer?"
column with a sureness
only my child-faith
might have touched.

Vintage Lot of Sunday School Invitations— 1960s

"A note to say—hope you'll be back in the swing of things next week"

Bunny on a swing,
bunny with a hat on,
bunny beckoning
back to learning. The
implication is you've
stopped swinging, are still
and sad. I don't think
I've ever jumped off
the faith swing set, but
I have, at times, been
still, confronted
with choice: to let
my legs pump in order
to soar, or let them
stride, successful
in abandon.

It's effort either way. Sometimes
pumping is more tiresome,
though. But there's still
some magic to not
touching the ground.

Fantastic Faith Tattoos—$2.57

*"72 temporary tattoos, including images of Moses,
Joshua, David, Deborah, Esther, and Joseph as well
as the words Trust, Believe, Pray!, Obey!, Strength,
and Power!"*

So many of my friends have real tattoos
that periodically I think about getting one
and whether there's anything I care about
enough to keep it on my body forever.

My imaginings tend toward faith
laced with the gruesome. Mostly
I consider a tent peg as a symbol
of Jael, who drove one through
an enemy's head in the book
of Judges. She, in her
glory, pierced me as well—
drove through my conception
that being a woman of God was just
one gentle thing.

It wasn't only her, of course,
but it is more poetic that way:
to say that Jael was the one
who shattered my head open,
so new ideas might fill
the fissures. Once those revelations
were stitched into place,
I knew fantastic faith.

Maybe I would have known sooner
if at seven I'd been sticking woman
warrior Deborah to my skin
or Esther, a savior of her people,
and maybe if they had been visible
next to a tattoo saying, "Obey!,"
it would've redirected every
obedient impulse toward the voices
saying to speak and stand.
Maybe I would've rejoiced,
pressing "Power!" to my cheek.

Antique David and Goliath
Board Game—1950s

"How to Win Goliath's Sword"

Alternative answers: win a spelling bee.
A singing competition, *Voice*-style
or *American Idol*, your choice.
Goliath is Blake Shelton. Goliath
is Simon Cowell. Maybe Paula.
Heave the sword out of the stone.
Challenge Goliath to checkers.
Chess, if you know how. Or
jump rope, if he can find rope
long enough. See who can go faster.
See who will not stop. Play darts,
but first, over the dart board, draw
a face, position it so the space
between the eyes is the center. Take
aim again and again. Filter out
the laughing bargoers and the giant's
trash talk. Do any and all of these
things with focus. Do anything
you can think of where you
might bloom big, gain size. Your
spirit may already be on its way
to meet his gaze in the sky.

Boasting Tower*

Instead of bricks,
I layer accomplishments.
Well, interpretations of them.
Accomplishments turned
into identities until I am
standing tall—someone calling
herself Empowerment,
Independence, Intellect,
Creativity, Whimsy, Determination.
A tower of the Jenga
variety, easily undermined
by a toying hand, withdrawing.
Is it a problem to build
or to lack cement?

*Title of a space on The Paths of Life board game,
published in 1840*

Jesus Has a Pizza My Heart
Notepads—$7.19

I get the pun, but
aren't we meant to give
the whole pie? There is reservation
here, restraint—suitable
for a Nicodemus type
coming to Jesus under the cover
of night. There is also
a realism. We hand out
pizza cutters, letting
others' words roll over
and over us until, finally,
they've broken off a piece.
Even the Peters of the world
sometimes deny him. So
maybe Jesus only has a pizza
my heart. If I can't give all
of it, let my offering still
be fresh and flaming, enough
to burn a lesser tongue.

Fall Faith Shape Stickers—$2.69

"I pick Jesus" written across
an apple tree, meaning Jesus
is the best in the bunch, the one
you want to taste before you even
leave the orchard, no other
loves managing his same shine,
no other apples so spoiled
that they could ruin him.
He asks for my reach, that
I'd stretch a hand into those
leaves and pluck. I wonder
if apples ever reach back.
If he's on a branch too high,
will he drop into my open hand?

Personalized Cross Mint Tins—$29.99

Jesus of the freshening.
Of the cleansing.
Of mouths transformed
and scents overcome.
Fit for a tin, thereby fit
for a purse or a car's
glove compartment.
Jesus, be easy as a mint,
as small. Cloak everything
in me that's wrong.

Personalized Cross Lollipops—$15.79

On this virtual corner that specializes
in the wholesome, you can buy,
for some reason, a lickable cross,
though no one can really call foul
when the Eucharist also means
taking the broken Christ
into our mouths.

What *is* the theology behind
crucifixion as candy?

I remind myself that there's a difference
between a crucifix and an empty cross,
the latter reminding that Jesus
no longer hangs there but resides
elsewhere, alive.

So maybe we should all be licking
toward eternity, even if the tongue
must pick up death's underlying flavor.
Candy a symbol of suffering
made sweet. A reminder that
divine intervention, on occasion,
might turn the worst to sugar.

Vintage "Be Thou Faithful" Sunday School Pinback Button—1940s

*"Do not fear what you are about to suffer. Beware,
the devil is about to throw some of you into prison
so that you may be tested, and for ten days you will
have affliction. Be faithful until death, and I will give
you the crown of life." —Revelation 2:10 (NRSV)*

The button does not include
the whole verse, only a reference
so someone could pull out a Bible
and learn that the wearer is steeling
themselves for what's to come;
also, learn what is coming. How old
were those who had this pinned
to chests, jackets, backpacks?
Reminder of suffering, but also
strength, a crown. Prophecy
serving like a child's tiara,
proclaiming, *The world will hurt me, but
for now, I am sparkling.*

Vintage Bible Astronomy Game—1920s

"4. Job's coffin or dolphin constellation"

The prompt makes no sense before
I turn to Google, where I learn
that a box of stars central to Delphinus,
the dolphin constellation, sometimes goes
by this biblical name. What versatility
written in the air. Both a creature,
alive, swimming through sea-sky,
and something more than dead:
inanimate—holder of death, buried and still.
The freckles that spot our bodies like stars,
do they all hold this same tension—
mapping both a readiness to dive
and the inevitability of hitting bottom?

$olomon'$ Treasure Game,
Game about Proverbs—1980s

> *"But it's more than a game. Players learn about the*
> *true treasures in life, including joy, happiness, insight,*
> *humility, knowledge, understanding, trust, and*
> *reverence for the Lord."*

When I try to trace back the origins of this
religious self, I remember a moment in the car—
Bible open in the backseat. My parents
asked what I was reading, expecting
the latest *Harry Potter*, but I answered,
"the book of Proverbs." In my teen
years, one AIM username declared me
Provrb1810meggy. "The name of the Lord
is a strong tower; the righteous run to it
and are safe." Sometimes I wonder why
Proverbs was my favorite, but I reread
that verse and know. I was afraid of so much.
Proverbs gave answers. Promises.
Wisdom simple and short. Faith reduced
to things I might win, benefits, self-
improvement: treasure. What now
do I name as treasure? What are the benefits
to belief if I've given up on being made wise?

Religious Fish Football Assortment—$13.09

God, give me a faith that can be tossed,
light in the air. Give me a faith that
I can catch easy. One of soaring
feelings, in the God who multiplied
fish beyond reason. Give me a faith
that is not scared of games or
the concept of playfulness.

Valley of Prayer*

I, too, am made
through rivers.

Life's erosion.
Despite these ways

in which I'm worn,
all earth's hills

are envious that
I (like all prayer)

nestle, nuzzle
the blaze.

My altitude defined:
as close as can be

to the heat that centers
and generates.

Title of a space on The Paths of Life *board game,
published in 1840*

Woman of Faith Soup
Mug & Coaster—$13.18

"You are a Woman of Faith"

I like the declarative quality.
Not "Be a Woman of Faith"
or "You can be," but "You are."
And not because you're doing
anything special or world-saving.
You're just sipping soup,
nothing achieved. Even in
the nothing, the neutral, maybe
faith still holds, you and
whatever keeps you warm.

Prayer Piggy Bank with Card—$29.19

If prayers are currency,
then they're pennies
found in couch cushions,
adding up over the years,
coins dinging against
ceramic like desperate
utterances dinging against
God's ear.

Imagine busting
that bank open, prayers
pouring forth.

Out in the open, you'll see them
for the lights they always were.

They'd been pulsing, hidden,
for so long from that place
on your nightstand,

as alive in the heaven you've never been to
as they were in the gut of that pig.

Vintage Bible Battles Card Game—1970s

The instructions allude
to Divine Intervention cards,
and I want to collect
all of them. Or: I want
to give them all away.
Or: I want to throw them
all out, after feeding
them one by one to
a shredder, so God can't
recognize my requests.
Or: I want to cover
them in glue, stick them
to my body, the grass
outside my apartment,
my cell phone, name
that She has intervened
here and here and here.

III.

Needy Maze*

Consider: a straight
line, tethering the self
to God, a friend,
a lover, for an un-
complicated system
of need-expressing
and need-receiving.
Consider how you've
never had it. Consider
that even speaking
at your plainest, in prayers
or texts or bedroom
whispers, the line
has always been cut
eventually. And yet
you still believe
you might find your way
to the other end,
to the one holding
what you're seeking,
even if it means
winding roads. Like
any mystic or unloved
romantic, you can
accept an elaborate
maze. You believe
in the possibility
of an unseen center.

*Title of a space on The Paths of Life board game,
published in 1840

Vintage Bible Pairs Make-It and
Play-It Game—Decade Unlisted

If we made it into scripture,
some twenty-first-century holy text,
would we qualify as a pair? Adam
and Eve, Cain and Abel, Jacob
and Esau, Noah and the Ark.
See, a pair doesn't have to be
positive or even all human.
It's about association, even
if antagonistic. Would we be a pair,
our stories lumped into one? Not
necessarily one of love but still—
acknowledged. Something to be
faced. Exegeted. A card that exists
to be played. I promise, I won't ask to win.

Jonah & the Whale Sign Craft Kit—$9.99

"Where are you going Jonah?
You can't hide from the Lord!"

Remember God is prowling, Jonah!
Remember also, whoever has this sign hung up
on their fridge, whoever put it together
with tiny hands. There is no room
of the house where He can't see you.
And He's looming outside too. You
can take a boat, a bicycle, an Uber,
but none will move swiftly enough
to outrun Him. But still, we say
it's good news—this scary surveillance.
The horror of always being seen worth it
if it means we can throw a worse
horror away: Jonah running further
and further until God disappears
from his life like an ex with whom it's finally
over, exactly what Jonah thinks he wants;
Jonah, meaning ourselves, facing
a reality where no one watches
or draws us back into their arms.

2020 Religious Water Color
Wall Calendar—$1.07

I like the picture
its months cast of
a delicate faith
found in flowers
and phrases like
"Grace Wins"
and "His Face Shines
Upon You" and
"All the Earth Rejoice."

There is no month
for Job. For Lamentations.
For "God, my God,
why have you forsaken,"
though that should
be the verse of the year.

A calendar is aspirational.
It imagines important dates
can be planned in advance,
their purpose clear
enough to be reduced
to a few words, a tiny box.

I can aspire to this: to their
March 2020, to "Sing
A New Song," to flowers,
to yellow, to straight lines
dividing each day from the next.

Many Friends City*

Imagine it on a map,
pointing you to your
next move: this is where
you'll find your happiness,
your people, be cared for
and loved. I had and left
such a city, and now,
even when I return,
it's like the name
has dissolved, like
the moniker has flitted
elsewhere, maybe
to another coast,
like someone is waiting
for me to throw out
the old map and buy
a new one.

*Title of a space on The Paths of Life board game,
published in 1840

Misery Square*

There are four points
that you cannot name,
but your life is lived
within them. Though you try:
perfectionism, single-
ness, the town where
you live, the human condition.
Sometimes you swap
one out for something
else. Sometimes you
accept that they are nameless,
that all that matters,
in the end, is the lines
connecting them, the way
they do not give as you push
at them from the inside.

*Title of a space on The Paths of Life board game,
published in 1840

Vintage Flannel Board Story
"The Little Foxes"—1950s

*"Catch for us the foxes, the little foxes that ruin the
vineyards, our vineyards that are in bloom"*
—Song of Songs 2:15

*"Place the body of the red fox, representing envy, in
the center of the board....the body of the gray fox,
representing selfishness, in the lower right hand
corner...the white fox, representing anger...the blue
fox, representing pride..."*

I declare I'm blooming
with the opposite of foxes:
generosity, selflessness,
calm, humility, honesty.
That I'm growing in virtue
and will continue as long as
the foxes stop sizing me
up with eager eyes. There
is always something ready
to nibble me down to sin.
Somethings plural. Someones.
Always alive, with teeth.

Bedtime Prayer Fleece Blanket—$5.07

I can hold off heartbreak
until 2 a.m., settling
into bed, remembering
that time you made me hope
for reversal.

If I marked them all off on a calendar,
what percentage of nights
would I find I've cried over you
these past few months?

There's utility in wrapping
this blanket around my sobbing
self—letting it pray for me.
"I pray the Lord my soul
to keep," because I only
want it back at sunrise, when
I know how to dilute longing
with all the distractions of daylight.

Family Blessing Wall Sign with Clips—$20.79

"family IS THE GREATEST blessing"

A thing that Jesus never said,
and his mother was Mary,
a generally agreed-upon
badass. For Jesus,
the greatest blessing
was losing, if we take
the Beatitudes at face value.
The most blessed person
likely walking alone,
persecuted and radiant.
And what would their wall sign
say? "God, take this blessing
away"? The same blessing
the prophets had,
to know God but not
enjoy him. That's not
the kind of blessing
this sign desires,
and I admit I don't
want it either. I want
a family of my own—
a husband, baby,
kitchen in which
to hang shlock like this,
a life that lets me believe in
a theology that cannot hold.

Gold God Gave Me You
Cake Topper—$5.17

*"Your faith in the Lord has been rewarded with your
perfect mate! Celebrate that blessing with this pretty
God Gave Me You cake topper, which will look simply
amazing atop your wedding cake."*

A few weeks ago I cried
over a country song about
praying for and finding love
because I missed believing
it works that simply.
Though, am I really
any smarter than I was
or just more cynical?

I cannot blame anyone
for putting "God Gave
Me You" on top of their cake.
I want to give God credit
for good things too. But I will rail
against claims of causation,
that those good things
are always reward,
because I will not accept
the inverse—that my life
is punishment, even
if I feel it.

Faith Arrow Sign—$11.09

That's all it is—the word "Faith"
under an arrow, leaving the consumer
to choose where it points. The
kitchen? So faith becomes
present in feasting. In the
hallway? So it becomes about
transition, faith the thing that carries
us from one room to the next.
To the bedroom? So faith
becomes what I touched
when he touched me,
transcendent. Faith, believing
without any evidence that
one day someone will be
beside me in that bed again.

Seduction Playhouse*

I liked when the game
involved yeses, kisses,

two winners, but now it's
evolved into who can best

push away desire, refuse
to grant the heart deciding

power. I was attracted, once,
to how decisive you were,

not thinking about all the ways
you might decide against me.

Title of a space on The Paths of Life *board game,*
published in 1840

Religious Valentine Conversation Heart Scented Erasers—$3.47

"SWEET ON JESUS"

I've wanted my love for Him
to erase all other loves. Not
because I'm devout but
because of the wounds.
I've yet to disappear,
these longings laced with pain,
though to be fair, I've never
put my whole weight
behind erasure. What more
must I give? What muscle
must I find? Though even
if I succeeded, what would be left
after all those loves were blotted
out to nothing? A blank-sheet
heart? Purity and emptiness?

The Resurrection Shaped Me
Putty-Filled Plastic Easter Eggs— 12 pc.—$7.28

Lord, make me as pliable as putty,
though only for the right hands.
Too many times I have given
myself to fingers rough
and ready to tear me apart.
And yet I believe this isn't
sin. It took a long time to realize
heartbreak isn't always wrong-
doing. Even now I know it
only in my head and not my body.
So I remind myself that putty
is meant for play, and likewise,
hearts for danger.

Vintage Come to Sunday School
and Church postcards, unused—1950s

"I saw a very lonely chair
At Sunday School cause you weren't there"

I keep the language of loneliness
cradled to my own chest, my own
thing to tend. I would hate
for it to be another's burden.
The postcard is bold
in its assertion. In blame.
Today I envy it, wishing
I could tell you just how
lonely you make me.

Let's Be Christian Soldiers:
Activity and Coloring Book—1950s

I am ready to detest you
until the Etsy listing
shows me your Joan
of Arc illustration,
and I am swept up
in a moment of
girl power feminism
and/or bisexual swooning
for my imagined
crush: Joan, the saint
I would date if I had
to date a saint. *Onward
Christian Soldiers*
becoming acceptable
if it's me and Joan.
Yes, let's. Me and
Joan both "brave, bold
heroine(s)," though I'll
wear a dress and let
my hair swing across
my lower back. I
would bumble on
battlefields but
could maybe match
her "flaming spirit,"
being both woman
preacher and drama

queen. Let's be
Christian soldiers
and never die.
Let's be Christian
soldiers and forget
also how to kill.
Let's be Christian
soldiers, enflame
our spirits with God,
with each other,
with tongue.

No Friend Shed*

Either a place of aloneness
or a motto about clinging, what
one isn't willing to lose.

The defining TV show
of my childhood featured
the line, "Lose one friend,
lose all friends, lose yourself."
I don't know if my younger
self thought that was tenable,
but since then, I've lost
so many friends—most to time,
others to conflict. Sometimes
I became more myself in the act.
"No Friend Shed" not an end-
destination. Not a home, not
even an apartment, but
a motel room you book
in a brand new town—a base
to return to as you check
out rental after rental,
search for the permanent,
ask, *What can I afford?*
and, when you feel brave,
Does it suit me?

Title of a space on The Paths of Life *board game,
published in 1840*

Growing Closer to God Women's
   T-Shirt—$7.97

On a T-shirt, a Bible with the words
"Social Distancing & Growing Closer to God"
on the front—proclaiming quarantine
a time to dive deeper into Divinity.

Where's the T-shirt that says
"Social Distancing &
Crying & Watching
Old Episodes of *America's
Next Top Model* to Fill
the Screaming Silence
& Texting My Ex-Boyfriend
Too Much & Wondering
How Long I Can Keep
Doing This &
Ordering Take-Out
Though The Internet
Says This is the Perfect Time
to Bake Bread & Donating
Money to Maybe Address Guilt
& Ordering Perhaps More
Alcohol Than Necessary
From the Local Coffee Shop/
Bar Doing Home Deliveries...
& Yes Maybe Even Growing
Closer to God, Knowing
God Is With Me Even in This,
Even Without My Normal

Worship, Without Bread and Wine,
Without Me Leading Prayers Up Front"?

The simpler route: adding, "This is maybe
the loneliest I've ever been," to the back
of the shirt, letting it hide behind a curtain
of hair until it peeks out via ponytail swish,

establishing truth one layer deeper,

not as contradiction
to the optimism emblazoned
across the chest,

just another fact that the God
I'm growing toward
already knows.

"Jesus Loves Me"
Pom-Pom Critters—$9.99

Little poofs with googly eyes
and sticky feet—the words
"Jesus LOVES me"
shooting out their sides;
otherworldly creatures
to remind, ironic, of God-made-
human. Sometimes I need
something outside my world
because my world is social
distancing and too many hours
in my apartment alone; is an
ex-boyfriend admitting
to feelings and three days later
saying we shouldn't be talking;
is a text from a man who
ghosted me and came back
and ghosted me again;
is me wondering, *Can I ever
be happy here?*, here
mostly meaning the town
I've moved to post-graduate
school, but maybe sometimes
just meaning earth. "Jesus
LOVES me," says my alien
friend, and for a moment, I am
there with the pom-pom critter
in a universe next door where

the creatures can't understand
my problems or maybe even problems
at all, where I'm wrapped in music
my ears have never heard, looking
at a horizon that those who broke
my heart have never shared.

Title Index

Symbols

A

B

W

First Line Index

T

W